WHEN I GROW UP

I'M GOING TO BE A MILLIONAIRE

(A children's guide to mutual funds)

Written by Ted Lea

Illustrated by Lora Lea

Printed in Victoria, Canada

Graphics and typesetting, Roy Diment
Vivencia Resources Group, Victoria, BC

Canadian Cataloguing in Publication Data

Lea, Ted, 1952-
    When I grow up I'm going to be a millionaire

    Includes bibliographical references.
    ISBN 1-55212-537-8

    1. Children--Finance, Personal--Juvenile literature. I. Lea,
Lora.   II. Title.
HG173.8.L42 2001   j332.024'054   C00-911417-3

TRAFFORD

This book was published *on-demand* in cooperation with Trafford Publishing.
On-demand publishing is a unique process and service of making a book available for retail sale to the public taking advantage of on-demand manufacturing and Internet marketing.
On-demand publishing includes promotions, retail sales, manufacturing, order fulfilment, accounting and collecting royalties on behalf of the author.

Suite 6E, 2333 Government St., Victoria, B.C. V8T 4P4, CANADA
Phone   250-383-6864   Toll-free   1-888-232-4444 (Canada & US)
Fax   250-383-6804   E-mail   sales@trafford.com
Web site   www.trafford.com   TRAFFORD PUBLISHING IS A DIVISION OF TRAFFORD HOLDINGS LTD.
Trafford Catalogue #00-0203   www.trafford.com/robots/00-0203.html

10   9   8   7   6   5   4   3   2   1

Table of Contents

CHAPTER ONE - TEN BUCKS A MONTH

Ellen and Griffin were walking to school. "What did you do last night, Ellen?" said Griffin.

"We rented 'Honey, We Shrunk Ourselves'. It was cool. Have you seen it, Griff?" asked Ellen.

"Yeah," said Griffin. " Sometimes I wish that would happen to my parents, so that I could do what I want to, like eat ice cream all the time."

"What did you do last night, Griff?" asked Ellen.

"I went to see my money coach." replied Griffin.

"What's a money coach?" asked Ellen.

"She's the woman who is going to make me rich!"

"How rich, Griff?"

"Well, by the time I'm about sixty I'm going to have a million dollars."

"No way! How do you do that?"

"All I have to do is put ten dollars a month in a special fund, and keep doing that until I'm over sixty."

"Wow! Just think of all the times you could go to Disney World with a million dollars!"

"Yeah, I wish I had a million dollars now. But who'd want to go to Disney World when they're sixty. We'll probably just want to sit in rocking chairs, and drink prune juice. But maybe I could take my grandkids to Disney World."

"I wish my grandparents would take me to Disney World. What if you put in more than 10 dollars a month?"

"Then I'll have even more than a million."

"I put ten dollars a month into my bank account," said Ellen. "So, will I be a millionaire when I'm sixty, too?"

The school bell rang, and children started running to their classrooms.

"We'll have to talk about this after school, Ellen. I can show you how to figure out how much you will have when you are sixty."

"I can't meet you after school. I have to go to the dentist. Yech! I hate it when they run that cleaning thing over your teeth. It makes your whole head vibrate."

CHAPTER TWO - RULE OF 72

The next day, after school, Griffin and Ellen met underneath the big oak tree next to the playing field.

A soccer ball rolled up between them. Griffin's sister, Janna, and Ellen's brother, Alex, came running up. "Come on and play soccer you two!" yelled Janna.

"Not right now, Jann, we're talking about something important."

"What could be more important than soccer, Griff?" replied Janna, as she and Alex dribbled the ball back to the field and their awaiting friends.

"So, tell me, Griff," said Ellen, "how do you figure you can make one million dollars, just by putting ten dollars a month away?"

"Well, it's just based on putting money away for a long time, and waiting for it to grow from a little bit to lots. It's all based on something called the rate of return, which is the percentage of what you put in, that is added to your money each year. If you get a higher rate of return, your money will grow faster."

"How do you figure out how fast it grows?"

"My money coach said it is all based on the rule of seventy-two."

4

"What is that? My grandmother is seventy-two. Does it have anything to do with how old you are?"

"No, not at all. The rule of seventy-two is based on how fast money will double, based on your rate of return. So, if you start with $100, it's how many years will it be before you have $200."

"How long does it take?"

"It all depends where your money is. For example, you said you put money in the bank. The bank pays interest every year for the money you have in your account. This is your rate of return for the year. Do you know how much interest your bank pays you?"

"I'm not sure, but I think it is about 3 percent."

"Really? That seems high. But, okay, let's say it is. So, three percent interest would be your rate of return in your bank account. This means if you have 100 dollars in the bank for a whole year, the bank will give you 3 dollars for the year."

"Why does the bank give you money?"

"The bank actually uses your money and lends it to other people, and gets way more money back from them than they pay you, but that's another story."

"So, what does this all have to do with the rule of seventy-two?"

"I was just about to get to that. What the rule of 72 says is that if you divide 72 by your rate of return - 3 percent, the result is the number of years it takes to double your money. So what is 72 divided by 3?"

"It's 24 isn't it?"

"Right on, so with your money in the bank at 3 percent it will take 24 years for your $100 to double to $200."

"Wow, that seems like a long time!"

"I think so too. But if you put your money in other places, you can get a much higher rate of return. For example, some places where you put your money may give you a rate of return of about 15 percent."

"Holy cow, that's a lot more than the 3 percent I get."

"It sure is. So how many years would it take to double your money at 15%?"

"Let's see, 72 divided by 15 - that's a tougher one. I think it's about 5 years."

"It's actually 4.8 years, but let's round it to 5 years. So in about 5 years your $100 will grow to $200."

"That's a lot faster than 24 years."

"It is. But how much would you have in 25 years at 15 percent?"

RULE OF 72

*72, Divided by the Rate of Return,
is Equal to Number of Years to Double Your Money*

Rule of 72 Table - Starting with $100

Rate of Return	3 percent	7 percent	12 percent	15 percent
Money Doubles after about:	24 years	10 years	6 years	5 years.
Money at start	$100	$100	$100	$100
After 5 years	$115	$140	$175	$200
After 10 years	$135	$195	$310	$400
After 15 years	$155	$275	$545	$800
After 20 years	$180	$385	$965	$1600
After 25 years	$210	$540	$1700	$3200

"Well, after about five years I would have $200. After 10 years it would double again and I would have $400, after 15 years $800, after 20 years $1600, and after 25 years, about $3200. Wow! That's a lot more than $200 after 24 years with a 3% rate of return."

"So, which would you rather have?"

"Well, that's quite obvious. But how about that million dollars? So far I've only got $3200. That still seems like a long way to go."

Just then, Janna came running up to them. "Griffin, we have to go now. Mom wants you to go home. You've got to practice your clarinet before your lesson."

"Darn," said Ellen, "just when it was getting exciting. Well, I guess I'll just have to wait for another day. See you tomorrow. Have fun at your lesson."

"Right, just what I wanted to do tonight, when Star Trek is on after school and I'll have to miss it. Just wait 'til I grow up and I can do what I want. Bye."

CHAPTER THREE - TIME IS ON YOUR SIDE

The next day, Ellen and Griffin were walking home from school.

"Did you see the Lakers and Raptors on TV last night?" asked Griffin.

"Yeah, that Kobe Bryant was incredible!"

"Yes, and Vince Carter was awesome!"

"He sure was. Hey, Griffin, can you tell me more about that stuff you were talking about yesterday?"

"What stuff, you mean about Star Trek?"

"No! You know I hate Star Trek! I mean how to make a million dollars."

"Oh yeah. You know one thing my money coach told me is that 'Time is on your side'."

"What does that mean, Griffin?"

"My parents told me that it was a song by the Rolling Stones."

"You mean those wrinkly old guys with gray hair?"

"Yeah, but I don't think that is what my coach meant. She said that kids have a huge advantage over adults - we all knew that anyway - because our money has a lot more chances to double over time. Our parents just don't have as many five year periods left as we do."

"Or those 24 year periods that I need with my money in the bank at 3 percent."

"That's for sure. I've just started putting in $10 each month, and in fifty years from now, when I'm about 60 years old, I'll have about one million dollars, if I can average a 15 percent rate of return."

"Wow, that's incredible. But what if you can't get that rate of return?"

"Well, even at 12 percent, I should have about $300,000 dollars at sixty, but I would have to wait for two more six year doubling periods - twelve years - to have over one million. I'll be over seventy then. Scary!"

"So how much of your own money do you have to put in over the 50 years?"

"Only about 6000 dollars."

"And you get one million dollars? No way, Griffin!"

"Yes way. I know it sounds hard to believe. But it's true."

"What if you put in more than $10 a month?"

"Well, Ellen, if I put in $20 a month at a 15% rate of return, I would have about 2 million when I am about sixty."

"Sweet. Does that mean your parents are going to have that much money when they are sixty?"

"No, I wish they would. Then they could give me a bunch. But my dad is 45, and if he started to put $10 a month in now, he would only have about $6000 when he is sixty, at the 15 per cent rate of return. Do you know how much he would have to put in each month to have $1 million when he is sixty, if he started now?"

"No, how much, Griff?"

"About $1600 a month."

"Is that at a 15 percent rate of return?"

"Yeah, and at a 12 percent rate of return he would have to put in over $2000 a month until he is sixty."

"Holy cow. Can he afford that?"

"No way! That's a lot of money."

"So, how do you get a 15% rate of return?"

"That's a long story. But my money coach suggested mutual funds."

"Okay, Griff. What is a mutual fund?"

HOW YOUR MONEY WILL GROW, IF YOU PUT IN TEN DOLLARS A MONTH (Depending on the rate of return)

Griffin's Age	Years Money is in Fund	How much Griffin puts in	Rate	of		Return	Griffin's Dad's Age
			15%	12%	7%	3%	
10 years old	0	$10/month					45 years old
15	5	$ 600	$ 860	$ 800	$ 700	$ 650	50
20	10	1200	2600	2200	1700	1400	55
25	15	1800	6100	4700	3100	2200	60
30	20	2400	13,000	9100	5100	3200	65
35	25	3000	27,000	17,000	7800	4400	70
40	30	3600	55,500	30,500	11,000	5800	75
45	35	4200	113,000	54,600	17,000	7300	
50	40	4800	228,000	97,000	24,000	9000	
55	45	5400	459,000	172,000	35,000	11,000	
60	50	6000	924,000	303,000	50,000	13,000	
65	55	6600	1,860,000	535,000	71,000	16,000	
70	60	7200	3,741,000	945,000	100,000	19,800	
75	65	7800	7,526,000	1,666,000	142,000	23,000	
			Doubles every 5 years	Doubles every 6 years	Doubles every 10 years	Doubles every 24 years	

15

Ellen looked at her watch. "Oh no, my mother is going to be really mad. It's 4 o'clock and I was supposed to be home at quarter to four. I have to go with her to the vet. Our dog has to get its shots. I'll have to hear about mutual funds later. Can you come over to my house tomorrow?"

"Sure, Ellen, see you then."

"Bye, Griff."

CHAPTER FOUR - MUTUAL SUPPORT

Griffin rang the doorbell at Ellen's house.

Ellen opened the door. "Hi, Griff, where have you been?" she said.

"I was just coming back from my first baseball practice."

"What did you do there?"

"Oh, my coach hit us some ground balls, and then more ground balls, and then more of the same. It was really boring. But then we got to hit. I was pounding them out into the outfield. That part was cool. He's a great coach - he is really positive and lets everyone play lots in every game."

"Awesome, Griff. I just got back from a soccer game. I'm really tired. It's a great game, always running, never boring at all. My coach is great too. She makes playing lots of fun."

"My sister, Janna, plays soccer too. She loves it."

"So does my brother, Alex. Hey, Griff, do you want a peanut butter sandwich?"

"Sure, Ellen."

"Then maybe you could tell me about mutual funds. You really got me interested in them. Tell me, Griffin, I wasn't clear about it when you left the other day. What is a Mutual Fund?"

"A mutual fund is something where a whole bunch of people combine their money for their mutual benefit, to own things to make more money for themselves. My dad says that it's sort of like taxes where everyone puts money in to buy something really big, like a bridge or a school. You know, something that one person couldn't buy on their own, unless they are really rich. Anyway, a whole bunch of people put their money together to buy a mutual fund. The difference from a bridge is that the individuals actually own the fund and can sell their part of it."

"Are these friends of yours?"

"No, mostly a bunch of people all over the country I don't know and never will know. Except my parents both have money in the same mutual fund that I have."

"So what happens with the money you put in the fund?"

"Well, there are a bunch of different kinds of mutual funds. Some are called bond funds, others are called mortgage funds, some are called money market funds and still others are called stock funds."

"What are all those things? Boy, there sure is a lot to learn in trying to make money."

"Yeah, I know. I don't know too much about most of the funds, but the one

18

I have is a stock mutual fund. My money coach told me that she thinks a stock fund is the best kind of mutual fund for me because I have such a very long time to invest, and that I might want to get the other types of funds later in life."

"What is a stock? Sounds like soup."

"A stock is when you actually own a part or a share of a company."

"What kind of company?"

"Well, you can own a part of all sorts of companies, like Disney or McDonalds, or Toys R'Us or computer companies or banks."

"Banks. My mom says banks always make too much money."

"Yeah, they do. That's why it's good to own part of a bank, instead of having your money in a bank account."

"If you own part of the company does that mean you actually are the boss of the people that work there?"

"Not really. You only end up owning a very small portion, and other people who have the same mutual fund or even other mutual funds also own a portion of the company. Only if you're really rich will you own enough of the company to be like the boss."

"Like when you get older?"

"Maybe, but that will take a long time. Anyway, Ellen, my mutual fund owns parts of a whole bunch of companies, and I own a little bit of each of them. Each year, some of the companies do well, and others may not do as well. But overall, my fund has had an average rate of return of over 15 percent, over many years."

"Does it ever have a rate of return below 15 percent?"

"Some years it is below 15, and some years it may actually lose money. But overall, good funds invested in the stock market have always gone up over the last fifty years. And it has gone up way more times than it has gone down."

"What is the stock market? Is that where you get soup stock?"

"The stock market is where people can buy and sell stocks. Sort of like a supermarket, only a little wilder. And prices can either go up, or go down. But over the long term, on average, they tend to go up if a company is a good company."

"When it does go down, does it scare you?"

"It might a little bit, but my money coach said that when the price of a stock mutual fund is down, it is a good time to buy more. It is like it is on sale and cheap. But it usually goes up again well beyond what it started from, before it went down. My dad says lots of people buy stock mutual funds when the price is really high, but that is a bad time to buy, unless you plan to keep it for a real long time."

"How do you know what fund to buy?"

Just then the phone rang. Ellen's brother, Alex, answered it. "Griffin, it's your mom. She wants you to go home right now. It's dinner time."

"Okay, Alex. I hope we have homemade pizza tonight. I guess I'll go home, as long as there is ice cream afterwards."

"We'll have to finish talking about this tomorrow. "

"This part is probably the most important part."

"What do you mean?"

"Choosing the right fund is very important, as there are some that are good and some that are not so good. But, I'll tell you more tomorrow. Bye, Ellen, see you then."

"Bye, Griffin."

TYPES OF MUTUAL FUNDS

STOCK FUNDS (also called EQUITY FUNDS) - best for children

A stock is where you own a portion or share of a company. These funds have a fairly high rate of return (yearly average over 10% if a good fund) over long term, but some years it may be quite low. You should keep these funds over a long period of time, for 10 years or more.

BOND FUNDS

A bond is where you lend money to a company or a government, and they guarantee that they will pay you back a certain rate of return each year, which is usually a moderate amount (6-10%), but fairly consistent. These are good to buy when you are an adult, as long as you have a fair amount of money in stock funds already.

MORTGAGE FUNDS

A mortgage is where you lend your money to someone to buy a house or a property, and they pay you back interest. These funds have a whole bunch of mortgages in them. Usually a moderate rate of return (5-9%), but steady. These are good to buy when you grow up.

MONEY MARKET FUNDS

This is the safest kind of mutual fund. Also known as cash funds, these are good to get for a short period of time, like a year or two. They have better rates of return than banks (3-8%). They include things like bonds, treasury bills, short-term loans to companies and governments, and cash. Good to have if you want to save to buy something fairly soon, instead of money in a bank account. You might want to have one of these when you are a teenager, and even as an adult.

BALANCED FUNDS
(also called PORTFOLIO OR ASSET-ALLOCATION FUNDS)

These have a combination of stocks, bonds, mortgages, and money markets stuff in a single fund. These are usually very safe funds, with a fairly good rate of return.

CHAPTER FIVE - THE RIGHT FUND

The next day Griffin and Ellen were eating their lunch together. "What do you have for lunch, Griffin?"

"I've got juice, a cheese and lettuce sandwich and some carrot sticks. What do you have, Ellen?"

"I've got yogurt, a sandwich and an apple. By the way, Griff, can we talk about mutual funds again?"

"Sure, what do you want to know?"

"Can you buy just a single stock or a piece of just one company, instead of getting a bunch in a mutual fund?"

"You can, but my money coach says you really have to know what you are doing, or you may lose a lot of money. Some stocks have a lot of risk in buying them. Mutual funds are a lot safer."

"Why is that, Griff?"

"Partly because of diversity."

"Diversity, is that like biodiversity?"

"I never thought of it like that, but I guess it's the same idea. Ecosystems are healthy if they have lots of different species in them, and if one is lost or does poorly, other species are there to take over. "

"I don't get the connection."

"Because stock mutual funds own parts of lots of different companies. If one or two companies have a bad year, and lose money, the other companies in the mutual fund will make up for them, and you won't lose all your money."

"You said partly. Why else are mutual funds safer than stocks?"

"Because the companies that run the mutual funds have women and men working for them, and all these people do is go around checking out companies to see if they will make money. So they know everything they can about the company, like what's going in and what's going out, and how healthy the company is."

"Sounds like a doctor."

"Sort of. But they usually know if a company will make money, and will be good to include in the mutual fund they take care of."

"What else is important in choosing a fund, Griffin?"

"Well, some funds only allow you to put $50 in at a time, but the company I use allows me to put $30 in at a time. Some funds let you put $20 a month into them."

"I thought you said you put $10 a month in your fund."

"In a way I do, but it ends up being $30 dollars every three months, because that's the lowest amount they will take. I guess they don't like to take small amounts of money. They probably just like people with lots of money."

"Well, maybe the companies will realize a lot more children will put money into mutual funds if they make it easier for us kids. I guess we just have to start getting more of us involved."

"Yeah, I don't know many kids with their own mutual funds. I think it is really cool. My dad says there are lots of adults he knows who do not have mutual funds either. Many more of them would probably start if they could put in $10 a month, too."

"Anything else to look for in a mutual fund?"

"One neat thing my dad has is an ethical fund."

"What is an ethical fund?"

"It's a fund that only buys stocks in companies that don't pollute the environment, or use child labour, or don't test their bad stuff on animals."

"Hey, that sounds like a great idea. How many mutual funds are there, Griff?"

"Umm, in Canada I think there are over 3000 funds, while in the United States there are over 10,000 funds, and there are all sorts of different kinds of funds."

"How do you decide which fund to choose?"

"Well, I think you really need help from someone who knows a lot about it. You should get a money coach. My money coach says it is really important to check out the funds yourself, too. You might want your mom or dad to help."

"How do you check out what is good, Griffin?"

"Well, there are papers and books and websites that rate how good each fund is. My mom showed me a bunch of books she got out of the library, which say what the good funds are. And my money coach said that you really should look at the rate of return a fund makes over many years."

"How many years?"

"You should look at the 3 year, 5 year and 10 year rate of return, and only choose those funds that are good for these times."

"Do some funds not give 15 percent per year?"

"Yeah, while some funds give you a 15 percent rate of return, others may only give you 2 or 5 percent."

"Wow, I wouldn't want one of those."

"No way, you have to be very careful."

"How high can mutual funds' rate of return go?"

"Some years some funds go up as much as 100 percent or more. But that is really rare. When they do, it is really exciting. Most of the time it just goes up steadily, and is just like watching paint dry."

"How did you learn about all this stuff, Griff?"

"You sure ask a lot of questions, but I guess that's the only way to learn. The guy who cuts my hair, Mr. Chilton, first told me about mutual funds."

"What did he say to do?"

"He said I should go see the lady who is his financial advisor. Some people call them money coaches, because they coach you how to learn to invest and make money. She is really nice. And she seems to know lots of things and she explained everything to me. She took lots of time with me and my dad, and told us all the options of what I could do with my money."

"I'll have to get her name from you. What else should I know?"

"Here's another good example for you, Ellen. My grandparents put one thousand dollars in a mutual fund for my sister, Janna, when she was born. If her fund gets 15 percent rate of return, she'll have over 4 million dollars when she is 60 years old, and 35 million dollars when she is 75 years old, and that's without putting any more money in after the initial $1000."

"That is awesome. Did they do that for you, too?"

"No, I wish they had, but in some ways, at least I know that my money will be something I earned and I'll become a millionaire all by myself. But my sister will probably want to start her own fund when she is ten, too."

"What if she adds to what she already has?"

"If she adds $10 a month, starting when she is 10 years old, she will have over 5 million dollars when she is sixty."

"Sweet, do you think she'll give any to you?"

"Only if I am good to her. Little sisters can be such a big pain."

"So can little brothers. Do you have any other advice, Griffin?"

"Always, Ellen. My money coach says it's really important that you should spend some of your money that you get from allowance or from working, and have fun with it when you are young, and at all other times throughout your life. And you can always try to make extra money doing things for your parents or other people, and add it to your mutual fund. My dad says that if I put any extra money into my mutual fund, beyond my $10 a month, that he will match that amount and put it into my fund as well."

WATCH THE GROWTH OF JANNA'S MONEY
STARTING WITH $1000 WHEN SHE WAS BORN

Age	12%	15%
At birth	$1000	$1000
5 years old	1750	2000
10	3100	4000
15	5500	8000
20	9650	16,000
25	17,000	33,000
30	30,000	66,000
35	52,800	133,000
40	93,000	268,000
45	164,000	540,000
50	289,000	1,080,000
55	509,000	2,200,000
60	897,600	4,385,000
65	1,582,000	8,818,000
70	2,788,000	17,000,000
75	$4,913,000	$35,000,000
	Doubles every 6 years (72 divided by 12)	Doubles every 4.8 years (72 divided by 15)

"Cool. But what happens if you spend the money in your mutual fund? What if you want to buy a bike when you're fifteen? Or a car when you are sixteen?"

"My money coach said that you should ALWAYS leave your long-term money alone, or you will end up using it and never have any for when you are older. So you should try to have a separate fund or way to save money that you can spend. She suggested a Money Market mutual fund for that."

"Is a bank a good place to put money?"

"Banks are good places to hide money so you don't spend it, but they are not good places to make money. My dad likes to call savings accounts 'losing accounts', because of inflation."

"Inflation, isn't that when you blow up a basketball?"

"Funny girl. It's something like that though, because it is something getting bigger."

Just then, the school bell rang.

"What do you get next, Ellen?"

"Math, Griffin - I love it! "

"I love it too - especially figuring out how many ice cream cones I'll be able to buy when I'm sixty. See you after school. I can tell you more about inflation then."

CHAPTER SIX - GOING UP OR DOWN?

Griffin and Ellen were walking home from school.

"Can you finish what you were saying about inflation?"

"Sure, Ellen. Inflation is how much the cost of things goes up. Through time it costs more to buy the same thing. Like if an ice cream cone costs one dollar this year, and next year it costs one dollar and five cents, then the inflation rate is 5 percent."

"My grandpa said that when he was young, ice cream cones only cost 10 cents."

"That's a perfect example of what inflation does to the cost of things through time. I sure wish I could buy a 10-cent ice cream cone. I'd buy about ten right now."

"What's your favourite flavour, Griffin?"

"I like Rocky Road or anything else with chocolate in it. What's yours?"

"I like vanilla."

"That's not really a flavour is it?"

"Funny boy! So, Griffin, what effect does inflation have on your money?"

"Well, whatever rate of return you make in the bank or in mutual funds means that the rate of inflation must be subtracted from it to figure out what you really get, because your money is worth less through time."

"Yikes, that's scary, so my money in the bank at a 3 percent rate of return, means that I would lose 2 percent if the inflation rate is 5 percent."

"Right, but fortunately the inflation rate is only about 2 percent right now."

"Yeah, but that means I am only really making 1 percent."

"Most bank accounts don't pay 3 percent interest. Many are at 1 percent a year or less."

"Wouldn't that mean that at a 2 percent rate of inflation I would be actually losing money in the bank at a 1 percent rate of return?"

"That's right. That's why you want to put your money where it will have a higher rate of return. Remember the Rule of 72. How long would it take you to double your money at 1 percent?"

"Let's see, isn't that 72 divided by 1? Hey, that's 72 years! That's almost my whole life before it doubles. I think I'll take most of my money out of my bank account."

"Unless you just want to hide it, so you don't spend it."

"Thanks, Griffin. Good advice. I better go now. We're going away for the weekend. We're going camping up in the mountains. It should be fun. We get to try out our new tent. See you Monday."

CHAPTER SEVEN - EDUCATION FOR THE FUTURE

After school the next Monday, Ellen and Griffin were talking about their weekend.

"Wow, we sure had a great time, Griffin! We did lots of swimming in the lake and we went on some really neat hikes. We saw lots of animals."

"Any scary ones?"

"No, fortunately not, but we saw frogs and deer and lots of squirrels. We sure saw lots of stars at night, before we went to sleep."

"Cool, I hope my parents take us camping soon."

"Griff, I sure have been thinking a lot about what you've told me about money.   Is there any other stuff I should know?"

"Well, let me think about what I've missed. There is so much to learn. One thing you and your parents might want to know is that there are ways your parents can save money for your education, in case you want to go to a university, college or technical school, when you're older. And it might reduce the amount of money they have to pay in taxes."

"My parents would love that. They hate paying taxes. How do your parents save money for your education, Griffin?"

"Well, our parents can save money in many ways, as long as it is being put away for our use. Mine put money away in mutual funds. My neighbour is about to go to college next year, and she said it costs so much to go there, so it is good for your parents to start saving early for it. Do you think you'll go to university when you are older?"

"I don't know what I want to do when I grow up. Not yet anyway. But I guess it would be good if my parents started saving. They can always let me go on a big holiday if I don't go to college. Do you think you'll go to college, Griffin?"

"I don't know yet either, but both my parents did, and they seem to think it would be a good idea. But my parents are happy that they can save from paying more tax by putting money away for my education, just like they can save from paying so much tax if they save in special funds for when they retire."

"Retire? Is that when they put new tires on their car?"

"No, that's when they quit working, and just sit around in rocking chairs."

"I hope I never do that. I just want to keep on running, which reminds me, I have to go now. My mom says she has something special planned for me for tonight, but she won't tell me what. See you tomorrow, Griff."

"Secrets! Well, I hope it is fun. Bye, Ellen."

COOL STOCK MUTUAL FUNDS FROM MANY COUNTRIES

You can buy mutual funds that allow you to own parts of companies all over the world. Make sure you discuss these with your money coach, before you decide the right one for you, as some of these may be risky.

GLOBAL (or International) FUNDS — **probably the best funds for children.** These mutual funds can buy stocks from anywhere in the world, including the United States and Canada, so they can pick from the best companies available. These include some of the best funds for long term growth of your money.

CANADA
Land of igloos, glaciers and high mountains (at least some people think that's all there is there - we know better). Usually slightly less rates of return than the United States, but fairly stable and steady growth for your money.

UNITED STATES
Very stable and steady growth for your money. Good place to buy mutual funds.

EUROPE
These are usually fairly stable funds with good long-term growth.

SOUTH PACIFIC AND LATIN AND SOUTH AMERICAN COUNTRIES
Less stable and risky, but over the long term might be good. You might want to get this kind of fund later in life, as long as you have many other kinds of stock funds, as well as bond, mortgage, money market and balanced funds.

CHAPTER 8 - WHAT IS REALLY IMPORTANT

Ellen caught up to Griffin on the way home from school the next day.

"Hi, Ellen."

"Hi, Griff. Guess what I did last night?"

"Was this your mom's surprise? What was it, Ellen?"

"I went to see a financial advisor and I started a mutual fund for 10 dollars a month. My older brother, Graham, started a fund too."

"Good for you. Maybe when we are both in our sixties, we can meet with our grandchildren in Disney World and talk about 'The Good Old Days', just like my grandpa does."

"You know, Griffin, one thing I have been thinking about is that it will be really cool having lots of money, but it is not the most important thing."

"What is, Ellen? Ice cream?"

"No, I think the most important things are friends, and family, and doing all sorts of neat things like learning new things, sports and going to cool places, even close to home."

"Right on, Ellen. I agree with you. Let's go have some fun!!!"

IMPORTANT TIPS FOR KIDS

FIND AN ADVISOR OR MONEY COACH THAT BOTH YOU AND YOUR PARENTS TRUST.

CHECK OUT THE FUNDS FOR YOURSELF BEFORE YOU COMMIT YOUR MONEY TO ANY.

MAKE SURE YOU LOOK AT AVERAGE RATE OF RETURNS FOR MUTUAL FUNDS OVER 3 YEARS, 5 YEARS AND 10 YEARS BEFORE YOU BUY.

DON'T EVER TAKE MONEY FROM YOUR LONG - TERM FUNDS.

PUT 25 PERCENT OF THE MONEY YOU EARN INTO LONG TERM INVESTMENTS, INVEST 25 PERCENT FOR BIG THINGS YOU WANT IN A WHILE (LIKE A BIKE), AND HAVE FUN SPENDING THE OTHER 50 PERCENT.

AS YOU GET OLDER AND HAVE MORE EXPENSES (LIKE BUYING A CAR OR A HOUSE) CONTINUE TO INVEST AT LEAST 10% OF WHAT YOU EARN.

ENJOY SOME OF YOUR MONEY BY SAVING FOR FUN THINGS YOU WANT.

DIVERSIFY YOUR FUNDS AS YOU GET OLDER, GET DIFFERENT TYPES OF FUNDS IN VARIOUS COUNTRIES AND HAVE A SIGNIFICANT AMOUNT OF YOUR MONEY IN SAFER INVESTMENTS.

ENJOY THE IMPORTANT THINGS IN LIFE - LIKE FRIENDS, FAMILY, NATURE, SPORTS, HOBBIES, HOLIDAYS, SCHOOL AND YOURSELF.

BOOKS AND SOURCES OF GOOD INFORMATION

THE BOOKS BELOW ARE MEANT FOR KIDS, AND FOR PARENTS TO HELP CHILDREN UNDERSTAND MONEY

Godfrey, Neale S. and Tad Richards. 1995. A penny saved: Teaching your children the values and life skills they will need to live in the real world. Simon and Schuster, New York. 240 pp.

Godfrey, Neale, S. and Carolina Edwards. 1994. Money doesn't grow on trees: A parent's guide to raising financially responsible children. Children's Financial Network Inc. New York. 175 pp.

Kyte, Kathy, S. 1984. The Kids' complete guide to money. Alfred A. Knopf, Inc. New York. 89 pp.

Pulver, Lana M. and Gail Kennedy. 1996. FIR$T CLA$$: The original financial guide for high school students. A Novel Approach. Raintree Communications Inc. 210pp.

AN AWESOME BOOK ON MONEY FOR TEENAGERS. 'THE WEALTHY BARBER' FOR HIGH SCHOOL STUDENTS.

Temple, Todd and Melinda Douros. 1994. Money-Making Ideas for Kids. A step-by-step guide to more than 40 creative and fun ways for your kids to earn money. Thomas Nelson Publishers. Nashville. 170 pp.

A COOL BOOK ON A BUNCH OF DIFFERENT WAYS FOR KIDS TO MAKE MONEY, TO BUY NEAT THINGS OR ADD TO YOUR FUNDS.

Vaz-Oxlade, Gail. 1996. The Money Tree Myth: A parents' guide to helping kids unravel the mysteries of money. Stoddart Publishing Company, Ltd. Toronto. 208 pp.

LOTS OF NEAT GAMES. A BOOK WITH GREAT ADVICE ON MONEY, HOW TO MAKE IT, HOW TO SAVE IT, AND HAS A GOOD SUMMARY ABOUT MUTUAL FUNDS THAT YOU MIGHT WANT TO READ BEFORE BUYING A MUTUAL FUND.

THE BOOKS BELOW ARE BOOKS THAT YOU CAN READ WITH YOUR PARENTS, AND YOU CAN HELP THEM PICK GOOD FUNDS FOR THEM, AS WELL AS FOR YOURSELF. AS WELL, THEY CAN HELP YOUR PARENTS DECREASE THE AMOUNT OF TAX THEY PAY, AND HELP YOU DO THE SAME, ONCE YOU START WORKING.

IN CANADA

Chand, Randa. 1999. Best of the Best Mutual Funds: 2000 Edition. Stodart Publishing. VERY GOOD BOOK. UPDATED EVERY YEAR

Chevreau, Jonathan, Stephen Kangas, and Susan Heinrich. 1999. The National Post: Smart Funds 2000. A Fund Family Approach to Mutual Funds. Key Porter Books, Toronto.

THIS BOOK TALKS ABOUT MUTUAL FUND COMPANIES AND THEIR FUND MANAGERS, AND THE VARIOUS MUTUAL FUNDS AVAILABLE IN CANADA. UPDATED EACH YEAR.

Kelman, Steven. 1994. *Understanding Mutual Funds: Your no-nonsense everyday guide.* Financial Times Personal Finance Library. Penguin Books. Toronto, Ontario. 201pp

GOOD BOOK FOR PARENTS ABOUT THE DIFFERENT KINDS OF MUTUAL FUNDS, HOW TO PICK FUNDS, AND HOW TO PICK FINANCIAL ADVISORS.

Moynes, Riley and Nick Fallon. 1999. *Top Funds 2000: Building Your Mutual Fund Portfolio for the 21st Century.* Prentice Hall. Toronto.

AN EASY TO READ GUIDE TO MUTUAL FUNDS IN CANADA. GREAT GRAPHICS THAT EVEN YOUR PARENTS WILL UNDERSTAND.

Pape, Gordon, Eric Kirzner and Richard Croft. 1999. *Gordon Pape's 2000 Buyer's Guide to Mutual Funds.* Prentice Hall Canada Ltd. Scarborough, Ontario.

A BOOK TO FIGURE OUT WHAT MUTUAL FUNDS YOU MIGHT WANT TO BUY IN CANADA, WITH A NEW VERSION CREATED EVERY YEAR.

Turner, Garth. 1999. *Garth Turner's 2000 RRSP Guide: How to build your wealth and retire in comfort.* Key Porter Books. Toronto, Ontario.

THIS BOOK MAY HELP YOUR PARENTS DECREASE THE AMOUNT OF TAX THEY PAY, AS WELL AS GET THEM TO THINK AHEAD.

Tyson, Eric and Tony Martin. 1995. Personal Finance for Dummies for Canadians. IDG Books Worldwide, Inc. 420 pp.

AN EASY-TO-READ BOOK, WITH LOTS OF GOOD ADVICE, AND TIPS ON MUTUAL FUNDS AND MANY OTHER FINANCIAL TOPICS

IN THE UNITED STATES

WITH OVER 10,000 MUTUAL FUNDS IN THE UNITED STATES, YOU NEED A BOOK LIKE ONE OF THESE TO FIGURE OUT WHAT ARE GOOD FUNDS WORTH PUTTING YOUR MONEY IN.

Kazanjian, Kirk.   2000. New York Institue of Finance Guide to Mutual Funds 2000.

THIS AUTHOR BOUGHT HIS FIRST STOCK WHEN HE WAS FIVE YEARS OLD. EASY TO READ. LISTS 1, 3 AND 5 YEAR RATES OF RETURNS FOR OVER 9000 MUTUAL FUNDS.

Walden, Gene. 1999. The 100 Best Mutual Funds to Own in America. Dearborn Financial Publishing Inc. United States. UPDATED YEARLY

Williamson, Gordon. 2000. The 100 Best Mutual Funds You Can Buy, 2001. Adams Publishing. Holbrook, Massachusetts.

THIS BOOK CLEARLY EXPLAINS WHICH FUNDS ARE VERY GOOD IN THE UNITED STATES, WITH A FIVE STAR SYSTEM JUST LIKE THE MOVIES (UNLESS YOU ARE USED TO THUMBS UP)

FOR ANYWHERE

Chakrapani, Chuck. 1994. *Financial Freedom on $5 a Day: A step-by-step strategy for small investors.* Self-Counsel Press. Standard Research Systems, Inc. Toronto, Ontario. 188pp.

DESCRIBES TO PARENTS HOW TO GET STARTED AND BUILD WEALTH OVER TIME.

Chilton, David. 1989. *The Wealthy Barber.* Stoddart Publishing Company. Toronto. 197 pp.

A GREAT EASY-TO-READ STORYBOOK FOR YOUR PARENTS, ON HOW TO SAVE AND INVEST YOUR MONEY

Hwoschinshy, Paul. 1990. *True Wealth: An innovative guide to dealing with money in our lives.* Ten Speed Press, Berkeley, California. 178 pp.

A BOOK FOR YOUR PARENTS WITH WONDERFUL INSIGHT INTO HOW TO BALANCE FINANCIAL AND NON-FINANCIAL NEEDS IN LIFE

WEBSITES IN CANADA *(just a few of many available)*
globefund.com;   quicken.com;   fundlibrary.com

WEBSITES IN THE USA
morningstar.com;   fundspot.com;   investorama.com;   buckinvestor.com;
findafund.com

THERE ARE LOTS OF OTHER GOOD BOOKS OUT THERE ON MUTUAL FUNDS. CHECK YOUR LOCAL LIBRARY TO GET MORE INFORMATION ON MUTUAL FUNDS AND OTHER FINANCIAL ISSUES, TO HELP YOU DECIDE WHAT MUTUAL FUNDS YOU MAY WISH TO PUT YOUR MONEY IN. NEWSPAPERS AND MAGAZINES ALSO GIVE RATINGS OF THE FUNDS EVERY ONCE IN AWHILE. THERE ARE MANY GOOD WEBSITES THAT LIST AND RATE MUTUAL FUNDS. THERE ARE ALSO SOME COOL COMPUTER PROGRAMS FOR FIGURING OUT HOW MUCH MONEY YOU CAN MAKE OVER TIME, AT DIFFERENT RATES OF RETURN.

ISBN 155212537-8

9 781552 125373